Kitty
and the birds

Story by Beverley Randell
Illustrated by Betty Greenhatch

Kitty is hungry.
Kitty is looking
for a bird.

4

Here comes a bird.

Here comes Kitty.

The bird is up in the tree.
The bird is safe.

The birds look down at Kitty.

"**Naughty Kitty!**
Naughty Kitty!
Naughty Kitty!"

Kitty is hungry.
"Meow, meow."

"Come in, Kitty."

"Here you are, Kitty."

Kitty is **not** hungry.

Kitty is up on the bed.

Kitty is asleep.